DAD'S
WIT AND WISDOM

QUIPS AND QUOTES FOR FANTASTIC FATHERS

RICHARD BENSON

summersdale

DAD'S WIT AND WISDOM

This edition copyright © Summersdale Publishers Ltd, 2018
First published as *Dad's Wit* in 2010

Illustrations © RetroClipArt/Shutterstock.com

Summersdale Publishers Ltd
46 West Street
Chichester
West Sussex
PO19 1RP
UK

www.summersdale.com

Printed and bound in Poland

ISBN: 978-1-78685-061-4

Substantial discounts on bulk quantities of Summersdale books
are available to corporations, professional associations and other
organisations. For details contact general enquiries: telephone:
+44 (0) 1243 771107 or email: enquiries@summersdale.com.

Disclaimer
Every effort has been made to attribute the quotations in this collection
to the correct source. Should there be any omissions or errors in this
respect we apologise and shall be pleased to make the appropriate
acknowledgements in any future edition.

CONTENTS

EDITOR'S NOTE

Head of the household or family cabbie? Breadwinner or barbecue-only chef? Soft touch or tyrant? A father has many guises and being a dad provides a lifetime of magical moments, from showing your little 'un how to score a goal in the back garden and being looked up to as a hero (commonly stops at about eleven years old!), to dancing the funky chicken at your child's leaving home bash and being the strong shoulder to cry on when things go wrong.

This collection is a celebration of why it's great to be a father. Even when they all seem to think you're just a bit silly, Dad always has wise words to impart. No one is too old to need their dad.

And for all those new dads out there, apparently the secret of successful fatherhood is 'to know when to stop tickling'!

FROM
HERE TO
PATERNITY

PARENTHOOD IS A LOT EASIER TO GET INTO THAN OUT OF.

Bruce Lansky

Oh, what a tangled web we weave
when first we practise to conceive.

DON HEROLD

Children are nature's very own
form of birth control.

DAVE BARRY

The problem with the gene pool
is that there is no lifeguard.

STEVEN WRIGHT

I feel cheated never being able to know what it's like to get pregnant, carry a child and breastfeed.

DUSTIN HOFFMAN

A ship under sail and a big-bellied woman, Are the handsomest two things that can be seen common.

BENJAMIN FRANKLIN

It is much easier to become a father than to be one.

KENT NERBURN

I like children.
If they're properly
cooked.

W. C. Fields

We have no children, except me.

BRENDAN BEHAN WHEN ASKED IF HE HAD CHILDREN

Why are men reluctant to become fathers? They aren't through being children.

CINDY GARNER

Is it to prove they had sex once?

JEREMY HARDY QUESTIONING WHY A MAN WOULD WANT TO BE A FATHER

I've got more paternity suits
than leisure suits.

ENGELBERT HUMPERDINCK

Every ten seconds, there is a woman
giving birth to a child. She must
be found and stopped.

SAM LEVENSON

Families with babies and families
without babies are sorry
for each other.

ED HOWE

L-PLATES

WHEN YOU BECOME A FATHER, YOU GET SCARED ABOUT EVERYTHING.

Alex Trebek

To be a successful father… there's one rule: when you have a kid, don't look at it for the first two years.

ERNEST HEMINGWAY

Babies are always more trouble than you thought – and more wonderful.

CHARLES OSGOOD

The worst feature of a new baby is its mother's singing.

KIN HUBBARD

It's like washing dishes, but imagine if the dishes were your kids, so you really love the dishes.

Chris Martin on why changing nappies is so rewarding

Some people have got advice, some people have got horror stories. I like people that look you in the eye with a glow and say, 'It's gonna be cool.'

RUSSELL CROWE ON IMPENDING FATHERHOOD

A baby is an inestimable blessing and bother.

MARK TWAIN

The most extraordinary thing about having a child is people think I'm a responsible human being.

COLIN FARRELL

When you are dealing with a child,
keep all your wits about you,
and sit on the floor.

AUSTIN O'MALLEY

The toughest job in the world isn't
being a president. It's being a parent.

BILL CLINTON

A father has to be a provider, a
teacher... but most importantly, a
distant authority figure who can
never be pleased.

STEPHEN COLBERT

THE GREATEST DAY OF YOUR LIFE

Although present on the occasion, I have no clear recollection of the events leading up to it.

Winston Churchill on his own birth

The way events are shaping, they'll be lucky to be present at the conception.

GEORGE H. DAVIES ON THE FUSS ABOUT FATHERS BEING PRESENT AT THE BIRTH OF THEIR CHILDREN

My daughter was born under a lucky star. Lionel Blair lived in the flat above us.

BOB MONKHOUSE

On the one hand, we will never experience childbirth. On the other hand, we can open all our own jars.

BRUCE WILLIS ON THE PROS AND CONS OF BEING A MAN

If men had to have babies, they
would only ever have one each.

DIANA, PRINCESS OF WALES

A home birth is preferable. That way
you're not missing anything
on television.

JEREMY HARDY

You can tell it's a journalist's child
because all he wants to do is to
drink and sleep.

JOHN HUMPHRYS ON THE BIRTH OF HIS THIRD CHILD

THIS MOMENT OF MEETING SEEMED TO BE A BIRTH TIME FOR BOTH OF US: HER FIRST AND MY SECOND LIFE.

Laurie Lee

All babies are supposed to look
like me – at both ends.

WINSTON CHURCHILL

THEY CAN IF YOU HIT THEM IN THE GOOLIES WITH A CRICKET BAT FOR FOURTEEN HOURS.

Jo Brand on the notion that men can't
experience the pain of childbirth

I remember so clearly us going into hospital so Victoria could have Brooklyn. I was eating a Lion bar at the time.

DAVID BECKHAM

Speech-making is exactly like childbirth. You are so glad to get it over with.

JOHN BARRYMORE

A little like watching a wet St Bernard coming in through the cat door.

JEFF FOXWORTHY ON THE BIRTH OF A CHILD

There is one rule, above all others, for being a man. Whatever comes, face it on your feet.

Robert Jordan

IT DOESN'T COME WITH A MANUAL

A truly appreciative child will break, lose, spoil, or fondle to death any really successful gift within a matter of minutes.

RUSSELL LYNES

Children really brighten up a household. They never turn the lights off.

RALPH BUS

Fathering is not something perfect men do, but something that perfects the man.

FRANK PITTMAN

The hand that rocks the cradle
usually is attached to someone who
isn't getting enough sleep.

JOHN FIEBIG

CHILDREN ARE LIKE WET CEMENT. WHATEVER FALLS ON THEM MAKES AN IMPRESSION.

Haim Ginott

The trouble with learning to parent on the job is that your child is the teacher.

Robert Brault

Did you know babies are nauseated by the smell of a clean shirt?

JEFF FOXWORTHY

There are 152 distinctly different ways – and all are right.

HEYWOOD BROUN ON HOW TO HOLD A BABY

Everybody knows how to raise children, except the people who have them.

P. J. O'ROURKE

A two-year-old is kind of like having a blender, but you don't have a top for it.

JERRY SEINFELD

I learned the way a monkey learns – by watching its parents.

PRINCE CHARLES

Child-rearing myth number one: labour ends when the baby is born.

ANONYMOUS

PARENTHOOD REMAINS THE GREATEST SINGLE PRESERVE OF THE AMATEUR.

Alvin Toffler

You can learn many things from children. How much patience you have, for instance.

FRANKLIN P. JONES

I WAS THE SAME KIND OF FATHER AS I WAS A HARPIST — I PLAYED BY EAR.

Harpo Marx

DADDY'S
LITTLE
PRINCESS

My finger may be small, but I can still wrap my daddy around it.

Anonymous

She got her looks from her father.
He's a plastic surgeon.

GROUCHO MARX

If I wanted something from my father,
I would put my little feet together
pigeon-toe style, tilt my head and
smile. I got what I wanted every time.

SHIRLEY MacLAINE

The first man a girl falls in love
with is her daddy.

ANONYMOUS

A son is a son till he takes him a wife; a daughter is a daughter all of her life.

PROVERB

I'VE LEARNED MORE FROM MY DAUGHTER THAN SHE HAS LEARNED FROM ME.

Antonio Banderas

'Margo, don't be a sheep. People hate sheep. They eat sheep.'

MARGO KAUFMAN ON HER DAD'S ADVICE AFTER SHE COMPLAINED TO HIM THAT SHE DIDN'T FIT IN

Nobody in this world can make me so happy or so miserable as you.

THOMAS JEFFERSON IN A LETTER TO HIS ELDEST DAUGHTER MARTHA

Little girls are the nicest things that happen to people.

ALAN BECK

It isn't that I'm a weak father; it's just that she's a strong daughter!

HENRY FONDA

When his daughter... says, 'Daddy, I need to ask you something,' he is... butter in a hot frying pan.

GARRISON KEILLOR

Though she be but little she is fierce.

WILLIAM SHAKESPEARE

FATHERLY
ADVICE

Never put anything on paper, my boy, and never trust a man with a small black moustache.

P. G. Wodehouse

My dad always used to tell me that if they challenge you to an after-school fight, tell them you won't wait – you can kick their ass right now.

CAMERON DIAZ

MY FATHER TOLD ME THAT IF I SAW A MAN IN A ROLLS ROYCE ONE COULD BE SURE HE WASN'T A GENTLEMAN UNLESS HE WAS A CHAUFFEUR.

Earl of Arran

I have found the best way to give advice to your children is to find out what they want and then advise them to do it.

HARRY S. TRUMAN

Never get a tattoo because if you turn to a life of crime you're easily identifiable.

AMY LAMÉ ON THE NUMBER ONE PIECE OF ADVICE THAT HER FATHER GAVE HER

My father always used to say that when you die, if you've got five real friends, then you've had a great life.

LEE IACOCCA

ALWAYS BE A LITTLE KINDER THAN NECESSARY.

J. M. Barrie

Ask your mother.

FRANK LANCASTER'S ADVICE TO HIS CHILDREN

Dad taught me everything I know. Unfortunately, he didn't teach me everything he knows.

AL UNSER JR

Father told me that if I ever met a lady in a dress like yours, I must look her straight in the eyes.

PRINCE CHARLES

Son, never throw a punch
at a redwood.

TOM SELLECK

My father was fond of saying, 'Better
to keep your mouth closed and be
thought a fool than to open it and
remove all doubt.'

CAROL THATCHER

My father used to say, 'Let them
see you and not the suit. That
should be secondary.'

CARY GRANT

Don't criticise what you don't understand, son. You never walked in that man's shoes.

ELVIS PRESLEY

MY FATHER WOULD SAY, 'DO THE BEST YOU CAN. AND THEN THE HELL WITH IT.'

Ted Kennedy

HERO
WORSHIP

Nothing could get at me if I curled up on my father's lap... All about him was safe.

Naomi Mitchison

You don't raise heroes; you raise sons. And if you treat them like sons, they'll turn out to be heroes, even if it's just in your own eyes.

WALTER SCHIRRA SR

I've had a hard life, but my hardships are nothing against the hardships that my father went through in order to get me to where I started.

BARTRAND HUBBARD

My daddy, he was somewhere between God and John Wayne.

HANK WILLIAMS JR

His heritage to his children wasn't words or possessions, but an unspoken treasure, the treasure of his example as a man and a father.

WILL ROGERS JR

For many people, God is just dad with a mask on.

ANONYMOUS

Dads are stone skimmers, mud wallowers, water wallopers, ceiling swoopers, shoulder gallopers, upsy-downsy, over-and-through, round-and-about whoosers.

HELEN THOMSON

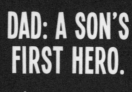

The father who would taste the essence of his fatherhood must… begin again beside his child, marching step by step over the same old road.

ANGELO PATRI

My dad is my hero. I'm never free of a problem nor do I truly experience a joy until we share it.

NANCY SINATRA

Directly after God in heaven comes a Papa.

WOLFGANG AMADEUS MOZART

I set the bar at half of my dad. If I could get that far, I'd consider my life successful.

Jeb Bush

CAN'T LIVE
WITH THEM,
CAN'T LIVE
WITHOUT THEM

THE ONE THING CHILDREN WEAR OUT FASTER THAN SHOES IS PARENTS.

John J. Plomp

What is a home without children?
Quiet.

HENNY YOUNGMAN

The soul is healed by being
with children.

FYODOR DOSTOYEVSKY

They are the greatest joy in the world.
But they are also terrorists.

RAY ROMANO ON HAVING CHILDREN

Having one child makes you a parent;
having two you are a referee.

DAVID FROST

Having children makes you no more
a parent than having a piano
makes you a pianist.

MICHAEL LEVINE

The trouble with being a parent is
that by the time you are experienced,
you are unemployed.

ANONYMOUS

Humans are the only animals that have children on purpose with the exception of guppies, who like to eat theirs.

P. J. O'Rourke

Insanity is hereditary – you get it from your children.

SAM LEVENSON

A doting father is not simply surprised when his little girl grows up;
he is crushed.

ANONYMOUS

The trouble with children is that they are not returnable.

QUENTIN CRISP

DEEP POCKETS

A boy becomes a man when he stops asking his father for money and requests a loan.

ANONYMOUS

It now costs more to amuse a child than it once did to educate his father.

VAUGHN MONROE

For the first year, you are only a curiosity… after that, an amusement park ride. Then, a referee. And, finally, a bank.

***ESQUIRE* MAGAZINE, 'THINGS A MAN SHOULD KNOW ABOUT FATHERHOOD'**

My daughter wanted a new pair of trainers. I told her, 'You're eleven. Make your own!'

JEREMY HARDY

A father is a fellow who has replaced the currency in his wallet with snapshots of his kids.

ANONYMOUS

A child, like your stomach, doesn't need all you can afford to give it.

FRANK A. CLARK

A truly rich man is one whose children run into his arms when his hands are empty.

Anonymous

A father is a banker provided
by nature.

PROVERB

If you want to recapture your youth,
just cut off his allowance.

AL BERNSTEIN

That is the thankless position of the
father in the family – the provider for
all, and the enemy of all.

AUGUST STRINDBERG

Life was a lot simpler when what we honoured was father and mother rather than all major credit cards.

ROBERT ORBEN

Well, it's hard to know what to get the man who provides everything.

MICHAEL FELDMAN ON RECEIVING A SET OF HOSE NOZZLES ON FATHER'S DAY

I want my children to have all the things I couldn't afford. Then I want to move in with them.

PHYLLIS DILLER

SETTING
A GOOD
EXAMPLE

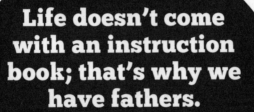

Life doesn't come with an instruction book; that's why we have fathers.

H. Jackson Brown Jr

Setting a good example for children
takes all the fun out of middle age.

WILLIAM FEATHER

My best training came from my father.

THOMAS WOODROW WILSON

My father taught me to work; he did
not teach me to love it.

ABRAHAM LINCOLN

Of course my father was a great
influence on me. He taught
me how to read.

MICHAEL FOOT

The father who does not teach his son
his duties is equally guilty as the son
who neglects them.

CONFUCIUS

Our father used to sit us on the po
and tell us ghost stories.

**BIG O TALKING ABOUT HIS FATHER'S ALTERNATIVES
TO LAXATIVES**

All children alarm their parents, if only because you are forever expecting to encounter yourself.

Gore Vidal

Children have never been very good at listening to their elders, but they have never failed to imitate them.

JAMES BALDWIN

Authority doesn't come from the loudest voice, but the wisest.

J. R. MORALES

Few things are harder to put up with than the annoyance of a good example.

MARK TWAIN

If you must hold yourself up to your children... hold yourself up as a warning and not as an example.

GEORGE BERNARD SHAW

Setting too good an example is a kind of slander seldom forgiven.

BENJAMIN FRANKLIN

You can teach better with your example than by your words.

REED MARKHAM

WHAT IS FATHERHOOD?

A FATHER IS A GIANT FROM WHOSE SHOULDERS YOU CAN SEE FOR EVER.

Perry Garfinkel

The secret of fatherhood is to know
when to stop tickling.

ANONYMOUS

I make it a rule to pat all children
on the head as they pass by – in
case it is one of mine.

AUGUSTUS JOHN

Up until I became a father, it was
all about self-obsession. But then I
learned exactly what it's all about:
the delight of being a servant.

ERIC CLAPTON

Being a father is like doing drugs –
you smell bad, get no sleep and
spend all your money on them.

PAUL BETTANY

There are three stages of a man's life:
he believes in Santa Claus, he doesn't
believe in Santa Claus, he is
Santa Claus.

ANONYMOUS

A father is a man who expects
his children to be as good as
he meant to be.

CAROL COATS

Being a dad is the new black.

Laurence Llewellyn-Bowen

Fathering is the most masculine
thing a man can do.

FRANK PITTMAN

Fathers embody a delicious mixture
of familiarity and novelty; they are
novel without being strange
or frightening.

LOUISE J. KAPLAN

Infinite patience, boundless
enthusiasm, kindness, the ability to
score a goal… and the strength to say
'NO' every now and again.

PIERS MORGAN ON WHAT IT TAKES
TO BE A GOOD FATHER

Fathers, like mothers, are not born. Men grow into fathers – and fathering is a very important stage in their development.

DAVID M. GOTTESMAN

Dads regard themselves as giant shock absorbers, there to protect the family from the ruts and bumps on the road of life.

W. BRUCE CAMERON

Chock-full of qualms and romantic terrors, believing change is a threat… like your first shoes with heels on.

PHYLLIS McGINLEY ON WHAT A FATHER SHOULD BE

SHE'S GROWING UP FAST!

I figure if I kill the first one, word will get out.

Charles Barkley on his twelve-year-old daughter's future boyfriends

A father is always making his baby into a little woman. And when she is a woman he turns her back again.

ENID BAGNOLD

The night I announced I was getting married, Daddy paced for hours on the porch.

LORETTA LYNN

I will look them up and down… I'll have the sword out and demand, 'What do you want from her?'

ANTONIO BANDERAS

Many a man wishes he were strong enough to tear a telephone book in half – especially if he has a teenage daughter.

GUY LOMBARDO

Daughters are like flowers: they fill the world with beauty, and sometimes attract pests.

ANONYMOUS

I have three daughters and I find as a result I played King Lear almost without rehearsal.

PETER USTINOV

Watching your daughter being collected by her date feels like handing over a million-dollar Stradivarius to a gorilla.

Jim Bishop

DAD VS MUM

You don't have to deserve your mother's love. You have to deserve your father's. He's more particular.

ROBERT FROST

You know the problem with men? After the birth, we're irrelevant.

DUSTIN HOFFMAN

Small boy's definition of Father's Day: it's just like Mother's Day only you don't spend so much.

ANONYMOUS

The most important thing a father can do for his children is to love their mother.

HENRY WARD BEECHER

Children always know when company is in the living room – they can hear their mother laughing at their father's jokes.

ANONYMOUS

My mother taught me my ABCs. From my father I learned the glories of going to the bathroom outside.

LEWIS GRIZZARD

Somebody said that no one can love a child the way a mother can. Somebody was never a father.

Anonymous

Mothers are a biological necessity;
fathers are a social invention.

MARGARET MEAD

I'm a fun father, but not a good father.
The hard decisions always went
to my wife.

JOHN LITHGOW

My kids hate me. Every Father's Day
they give a 'World's Greatest Dad'
mug to the milkman.

RODNEY DANGERFIELD

A GOOD FATHER IS A LITTLE BIT OF A MOTHER.

Lee Salk

GROWING
PAINS

A lot of parents pack up their troubles and send them off to summer camp.

Raymond Duncan

No man should bring children into the world who is unwilling to persevere to the end in their nature and education.

PLATO

THE CHILDREN DESPISE THEIR PARENTS UNTIL THE AGE OF FORTY, WHEN THEY SUDDENLY BECOME JUST LIKE THEM THUS PRESERVING THE SYSTEM.

Quentin Crewe

A child enters your home… makes so
much noise you can hardly stand it.
The child departs, leaving the house
so silent you think you are going mad.

JOHN ANDREW HOLMES

The worst waste of breath,
next to playing a saxophone,
is advising a son.

KIN HUBBARD

We spend the first year of a child's life
teaching it to walk and talk and the
rest of its life to shut up and sit down.

NEIL DeGRASSE TYSON

Parents were invented to make children happy by giving them something to ignore.

OGDEN NASH

Cleaning your house while your kids are still growing is like shovelling the sidewalk before it stops snowing.

PHYLLIS DILLER

Never underestimate a child's ability to get into more trouble.

MARTIN MULL

You know... children are growing up
when they stop asking... where they
came from and refuse to tell
you where they're going.

P. J. O'ROURKE

Your children tell you casually years
later what it would have killed you
with worry to know at the time.

MIGNON McLAUGHLIN

It's occasionally maddening to see
your children doing the things that
you did that were stupid.

GEORGE MARTIN

Don't try to make children grow up to be like you, or they may do it.

Russell Baker

THE BEST
JOB IN
THE WORLD

Happiness is having a large, loving, caring, close-knit family in another city.

GEORGE BURNS

WHAT'S A GOOD INVESTMENT? GO HOME FROM WORK EARLY AND SPEND THE AFTERNOON THROWING A BALL AROUND WITH YOUR SON.

Ben Stein

There's a time for being a rock star, on TV, and in the studio, but you've got to put time aside for being daddy, and getting chocolate rubbed in your face.

NOEL GALLAGHER

BEING A DAD IS MORE IMPORTANT THAN FOOTBALL.

David Beckham

I've made a few nice dishes in my time, but this has got to be the best one I've ever made.

JAMIE OLIVER TALKING ABOUT HIS FIRST CHILD

I figure somewhere between kid number one and number seven, I must have learned a few things.

MEL GIBSON

Anyone who hasn't had children doesn't know what life is.

HENRY MILLER

A three-year-old child... gets almost as much fun out of a... set of swings as it does out of finding a small green worm.

Bill Vaughan

FAMILY
MAN

HAVING A FAMILY IS LIKE HAVING A BOWLING ALLEY INSTALLED IN YOUR HEAD.

Martin Mull

I've got seven kids. The three words you hear most around my house are 'hello', 'goodbye' and 'I'm pregnant'.

DEAN MARTIN

Families are like fudge – mostly sweet with a few nuts.

ANONYMOUS

Character is largely caught, and the father and the home should be the great sources of character infection.

FRANK H. CHELEY

You don't choose your family.
They are God's gift to you,
as you are to them.

DESMOND TUTU

Raising children is like making
biscuits: it is as easy to raise a big
batch as one, while you have your
hands in the dough.

E. W. HOWE

A man that doesn't spend time with
his family can never be a real man.

MARIO PUZO

There is no cure for laziness but a large family helps.

Herbert Prochnow

A HAPPY FAMILY IS BUT AN EARLIER HEAVEN.

George Bernard Shaw

Family life is a bit like a runny
peach pie – not perfect but
who's complaining?

ROBERT BRAULT

Before I got married I had six theories
about bringing up children; now I
have six children, and no theories.

JOHN WILMOT

A family is a unit composed…
of children… men, women,
an occasional animal, and
the common cold.

OGDEN NASH

When our relatives are at home, we have to think of all their good points or it would be impossible to endure them.

GEORGE BERNARD SHAW

Children are a great comfort in your old age – and they help you reach it faster, too.

LIONEL KAUFFMAN

When you have kids, it takes the focus off you. You forget about what clothes you're wearing, or if you went to the gym.

JAMES DENTON

HEY,
BABY!

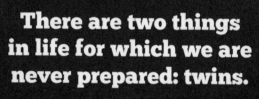

There are two things in life for which we are never prepared: twins.

Josh Billings

Breastfeeding should not be attempted by fathers with hairy chests... they can make the baby sneeze.

MIKE HARDING

Typical of Margaret. She produced twins and avoided the necessity of a second pregnancy.

DENIS THATCHER

I spoke to Luca on the phone and he burped, I was in tears. He looks like a turnip, but a beautiful turnip.

COLIN FIRTH

The toddler craves independence,
but he fears desertion.

DOROTHY CORKILLE BRIGGS

Babies are the enemies of
the human race.

ISAAC ASIMOV

Here we have a baby. It is composed
of a bald head and a pair of lungs.

EUGENE FIELD

A LOUD NOISE AT ONE END AND NO SENSE OF RESPONSIBILITY AT THE OTHER.

Ronald Knox's definition of a baby

Having children gives your life a purpose. Right now, my purpose is to get some sleep.

RENO GOODALE

Having a baby changes the way you view your in-laws. I love it when they come to visit now. They can hold the baby and I can go out.

MATTHEW BRODERICK

'Diaper' backwards spells 'repaid'. Think about it.

MARSHALL McLUHAN

TEENAGE
KICKS

Teenagers are God's punishment for having sex.

Patrick Murray

Few things are more satisfying than seeing your children have teenagers of their own.

DOUG LARSON

Let your child be the teenager he or she wants to be, not the adolescent you were or wish you had been.

LAURENCE STEINBERG AND ANN LEVINE

Adolescence begins when children stop asking questions – because they know all the answers.

EVAN ESAR

An adolescent is somebody who is in between things. A teenager is somebody who's kind of permanently there.

ANDREW GREELEY

It's amazing. One day you look at your phone bill and realise they're teenagers.

MILTON BERLE

The main problem with teenagers is that they're just like their parents were at their age.

ANONYMOUS

TEENAGERS. EVERYTHING IS SO APOCALYPTIC.

Kami Garcia

When you are seventeen you aren't really serious.

ARTHUR RIMBAUD

THE YOUNG ALWAYS HAVE THE SAME PROBLEM — HOW TO REBEL AND CONFORM AT THE SAME TIME.

Quentin Crisp

Telling a teenager the facts of life is
like giving a fish a bath.

ARNOLD H. GLASOW

Imagination is something that sits up
with Dad and Mum the first time their
teenager stays out late.

LANE OLINGHOUSE

Raising teenagers is like
nailing jelly to a tree.

ANONYMOUS

PARENTING
101

Most children threaten at times to run away from home. This is the only thing that keeps some parents going.

Phyllis Diller

Always have a change of shirt in the car – one that blends with spit-up is a good choice!

BRIDGET MOYNAHAN

If you want your children to listen, try talking softly – to someone else.

ANN LANDERS

Parents… spend half their time wondering how their children will turn out, and the rest… when they will turn in.

ELEANOR GRAHAM VANCE

Allow children to be happy in their own way, for what better way will they find?

SAMUEL JOHNSON

Don't worry that children never listen to you; worry that they are always watching you.

ROBERT FULGHUM

There's no road map on how to raise a family: it's always an enormous negotiation.

MERYL STREEP

Just do your job right and your
kids will love you.

ETHEL WATERS

Children behave as well as
they are treated.

JAN HUNT

I just take it hour by hour.

DEBRA MESSING

Children are unpredictable. You never know what inconsistency they're going to catch you in next.

FRANKLIN P. JONES

A child's mind is not a container to be filled but rather a fire to be kindled.

DOROTHEA BRANDE

The kids who need the most love will ask for it in the most unloving ways.

RUSSELL BARKLEY

To bring up a child in
the way he should go,
travel that way yourself
once in a while.

Josh Billings

LIKE
FATHER,
LIKE SON

A man's children and his garden both reflect the amount of weeding done during the growing season.

ANONYMOUS

MOTHER WOULD COME OUT AND SAY, 'YOU'RE TEARING UP THE GRASS.' 'WE'RE NOT RAISING GRASS,' DAD WOULD REPLY. 'WE'RE RAISING BOYS.'

Harmon Killebrew on playing rough with his dad

William Pitt the Younger is not only a chip off the old block but the old block itself.

EDMUND BURKE

All my sons are named George Foreman. They all know where they came from.

GEORGE FOREMAN

For rarely are sons similar to their fathers: most are worse, and a few are better than their fathers.

HOMER

MY FATHER HAD A PROFOUND INFLUENCE ON ME; HE WAS A LUNATIC.

Spike Milligan

It is not flesh and blood but the heart which makes us fathers and sons.

Friedrich Schiller

When you can't do anything else to a boy, you can make him wash his face.

E. W. HOWE

Fathers and sons show much more consideration towards one another than mothers and daughters do.

FRIEDRICH NIETZSCHE

I don't mind looking into the mirror and seeing my father.

MICHAEL DOUGLAS

Dad always called me his 'favourite son'.

CAMERON DIAZ ON BEING A TOMBOY

MANY FATHERS… HAVE EXPERIENCED THE CRUELLEST, MOST CRUSHING REJECTION OF ALL: THEIR CHILDREN HAVE ENDED UP SUPPORTING THE WRONG TEAM.

Nick Hornby

MY WISE
OLD MAN

My father gave me these hints on speech-making: 'Be sincere… be brief… be seated.'

JAMES ROOSEVELT

MY SON COMPLAINS ABOUT HEADACHES. I TELL HIM ALL THE TIME, WHEN YOU GET OUT OF BED, IT'S FEET FIRST!

Henny Youngman

Dad always thought that laughter was the best medicine, which… is why several of us died of tuberculosis.

JACK HANDEY

Jarrell was not so much a father… as an affectionate encyclopaedia.

MARY JARRELL

By the time a man realises that maybe his father was right, he usually has a son who thinks he's wrong.

CHARLES WADSWORTH

Parents can only give good advice or put them on the right paths.

Anne Frank

My father considered a walk among
the mountains as the equivalent
of churchgoing.

ALDOUS HUXLEY

I HAVE ALWAYS HAD THE FEELING I COULD DO ANYTHING AND MY DAD TOLD ME I COULD. I WAS IN COLLEGE BEFORE I FOUND OUT HE MIGHT BE WRONG.

Ann Richards

I have never been a material girl. My father always told me never to love anything that cannot love you back.

IMELDA MARCOS

As daddy said, life is ninety-five per cent anticipation.

GLORIA SWANSON

My dad always had this little sign on his desk: 'The bigger your head is, the easier your shoes are to fill.'

PHIL JACKSON

NO. 1 DAD

Dads grab themselves a spoon and
dig right in with you.

ANONYMOUS

Your dad is the man who does... the
heavy shovelling for your sandcastle,
and then tells you you've done a
wonderful job.

ROSE O'KELLY

He sewed button eyes on my teddy
bear when its other eyes fell off.

CYNTHIA HEIMEL

When I was a kid, I used to imagine animals running under my bed. I told my dad… He cut the legs off the bed.

LOU BROCK

Being a great father is like shaving. No matter how good you shaved today, you have to do it again tomorrow.

REED MARKHAM

What do I owe my father? Everything.

HENRY VAN DYKE

I LOOKED UP TO MY DAD. HE WAS ALWAYS ON A LADDER.

David Chartrand

He sat there and ate in the pouring rain, dripping wet, just for the hell of it.

Dick Van Dyke on his dad at a family picnic

I talk to him secretly not really knowing whether he hears, but it makes me feel better.

NATASHA JOSEFOWITZ ON TALKING TO HER DECEASED FATHER

None of you can ever be proud enough of being the child of such a father who has not his equal in this world – so great, so good, so faultless.

QUEEN VICTORIA

I think my dad is a lot cooler than other dads. He acts like he's still seventeen.

MILEY CYRUS

HE OPENED THE JAR OF PICKLES WHEN NO ONE ELSE COULD.

Erma Bombeck

TOUGH
LOVE

My father only hit me once –
but he used a Volvo.

BOB MONKHOUSE

MY MOTHER PROTECTED ME FROM THE WORLD, AND MY FATHER THREATENED ME WITH IT.

Quentin Crisp

Raising kids is part joy and part guerrilla warfare.

ED ASNER

One motivation is worth ten threats, two pressures and six reminders.

PAUL SWEENEY

My father bought me a blunt instrument. He told me to knock myself out.

JAY LONDON ON THE TIME HE TOLD HIS DAD HE WANTED TO TAKE UP MUSIC

Never raise your hand to your kids.
It leaves your groin unprotected.

RED BUTTONS

The sooner you treat your son as a
man, the sooner he will be one.

JOHN DRYDEN

I find that waving the gun around
pretty much gets the same job done.

**DENIS LEARY ON HIS REFUSAL TO SMACK
HIS CHILDREN**

I never got along with my dad. Kids used to come up to me and say, 'My dad can beat up your dad.' I'd say, 'Yeah? When?'

BILL HICKS

CHILDREN ARE GLEEFUL BARBARIANS.

Joseph Morgenstern

FATHER'S PRIDE

She's more beautiful than the Brooklyn Bridge!

Charles Hayes on first seeing his child Mary

Children are the only form of immortality that we can be sure of.

PETER USTINOV

One of the greatest titles in the world is parent.

JIM DeMINT

Love and fear. Everything the father of a family says must inspire one or the other.

JOSEPH JOUBERT

My father gave me the greatest gift
anyone could give another person:
he believed in me.

JIM VALVANO

Getting a burp out of your little thing
is probably the greatest satisfaction
I've come across.

BRAD PITT ON HIS FIRST CHILD

When you have brought up kids,
there are memories you store
directly in your tear ducts.

ROBERT BRAULT

TO ME, HAVING KIDS IS THE ULTIMATE JOB IN LIFE.

Nick Lachey

While we try to teach our children all about life, our children teach us what life is all about.

ANGELA SCHWINDT

By profession, I am a soldier and take pride in that fact. But I am prouder, infinitely prouder, to be a father.

GENERAL DOUGLAS MacARTHUR

Once I had my first hit, Dad started to introduce himself as Nancy Sinatra's father!

NANCY SINATRA

DAD'S IN CHARGE

Well I'm his daddy... so he answers to me first.

Kevin Millar

A father's words are like a thermostat that sets the temperature in the house.

PAUL LEWIS

Always obey your parents, when they are present.

MARK TWAIN

The voice of parents is the voice of gods, for to their children they are heaven's lieutenants.

WILLIAM SHAKESPEARE

Parents who are afraid to put their foot down usually have children who step on their toes.

PROVERB

My dad is my best friend, my father, and my boss. When I do something... he likes... it feels three times as good.

DAVID LAUREN

We all knew Dad was the one in charge: he had control of the remote.

ANONYMOUS

PARENTS ARE THE BONES ON WHICH CHILDREN SHARPEN THEIR TEETH.

Peter Ustinov

You hate to say things that
will upset your kids, but then
sometimes you have to because
you can't let them run
around wild.

OZZY OSBOURNE

MY FATHER WAS AFRAID OF HIS FATHER, I WAS AFRAID OF MY FATHER, AND I DON'T SEE WHY MY CHILDREN SHOULDN'T BE AFRAID OF ME.

Lord Mountbatten

If your children look up to you, you've made a success of life's biggest job.

Anonymous

SPORTS
MAD DAD

'WHAT HE CAN'T LEARN
ON THE BACK OF A
HORSE IS NOT
WORTH TEACHING.'

Dick Francis quoting his father

A father's solemn duty is to watch
football with his children and teach
them when to shout at the ref.

PAUL COLLINS

The place of the father in the modern
suburban family is a very small one,
particularly if he plays golf.

BERTRAND RUSSELL

It is admirable for a man to take his
son fishing, but there is a special
place in heaven for the father who
takes his daughter shopping.

JOHN SINOR

It's not the fishin'… It's the time together.

ANONYMOUS

If you put a baseball and other toys in front of a baby, he'll pick up a baseball in preference to the others.

TRIS SPEAKER

There are three things in my life which I really love: God, my family, and baseball… Once baseball season starts, I change the order around a bit.

AL GALLAGHER

'Dad, what do people do on Sunday who don't play golf?'

Bobby Jones to his father as a child

DADDY OR CHIPS?

This would be a better world
for children if the parents had
to eat the spinach.

GROUCHO MARX

A COMPROMISE IS THE ART OF DIVIDING A CAKE IN SUCH A WAY THAT EVERYONE BELIEVES HE HAS THE BIGGEST PIECE.

Ludwig Erhard

THE OTHER NIGHT I ATE AT A REALLY NICE FAMILY RESTAURANT. EVERY TABLE HAD AN ARGUMENT GOING.

George Carlin

Kids are great. They never know
when I steal a few of their sweeties.

ANONYMOUS

There are times when parenthood
seems nothing but feeding the
mouth that bites you.

PETER DE VRIES

My father was a fastidious man.
He ate a banana with a
knife and fork.

QUENTIN CRISP

My dad was a mean man, he hypnotised my mother not to order a starter.

HARRY HILL

GOVERN A FAMILY AS YOU WOULD COOK A SMALL FISH — VERY GENTLY.

Proverb

As a child my family's menu consisted of two choices: take it or leave it.

Buddy Hackett

ALL YOU NEED IS LOVE

There's no pillow quite so soft as a
father's strong shoulder.

RICHARD L. EVANS

We never know the love of a parent
till we become parents ourselves.

HENRY WARD BEECHER

I am not ashamed to say that no man
I ever met was my father's equal, and
I never loved any other man as much.

HEDY LAMARR

I love my dad, although I'm definitely critical of him sometimes, like when his pants are too tight.

LIV TYLER

I cannot understand how in the past I managed to cope without getting cuddled this many times a day.

RUSSELL CROWE

Stop trying to perfect your child, but keep trying to perfect your relationship with him.

DR HENKER

LET YOUR CHILDREN GO IF YOU WANT TO KEEP THEM.

Malcolm Stevenson Forbes

Fatherly love is the ability to expect the best from your children despite the facts.

Jasmine Birtles

Men love their children, not because they are promising plants, but because they are theirs.

CHARLES MONTAGU

Children need love, especially when they don't deserve it.

HAROLD HULBERT

I loved my father. I looked for his faithful response in the eyes of many men.

PATRICIA NEAL

DAD'S TAXI SERVICE

A pedestrian… is a man who has two cars – one being driven by his wife and the other by one of his children.

ROBERT BRADBURY

THE FATHER IS CONCERNED WITH PARKING SPACE, THE CHILDREN WITH OUTER SPACE AND THE MOTHER WITH CLOSET SPACE.

Evan Esar

Can you abandon a child along a public highway for kicking daddy's seat for 600 miles?

Erma Bombeck

Children in the back seat of cars
cause accidents. And accidents
in the back seats of cars
cause children.

SID CAESAR

IT IS AMAZING HOW QUICKLY THE KIDS LEARN TO DRIVE A CAR, YET ARE UNABLE TO UNDERSTAND THE LAWNMOWER... OR VACUUM CLEANER.

Ben Bergor

A FATHER AND HIS CAR KEYS ARE SOON PARTED.

Anonymous

DAD, YOU'RE SO EMBARRASSING!

Sing out loud in the car even, or especially, if it embarrasses your children.

Marilyn Penland

Because of their size, parents may be difficult to discipline properly.

P. J. O'ROURKE

If my dad didn't think they were funny, he wouldn't let them in the house.

MIKE MYERS ON THE WAY HIS DAD TREATED HIS FRIENDS

My father hated radio and he could not wait for television to be invented so that he could hate that too.

PETER DE VRIES

I was always embarrassed because my dad wore a suit… while my friends' parents were punks or hippies.

SHIRLEY MANSON

I'M PROBABLY GOING TO BE ONE OF THOSE VERY EMBARRASSING PARENTS WHO'S A NATURIST.

Robbie Williams

TO AN ADOLESCENT, THERE IS NOTHING IN THE WORLD MORE EMBARRASSING THAN A PARENT.

Dave Barry

If you're interested in finding out more about our books, find us on Facebook at **Summersdale Publishers** and follow us on Twitter at **@Summersdale**.

www.summersdale.com